# FROM PRISON TO THE PULPIT

# *MY TESTIMONY*

## JERMAINE JOHNSON

ISBN: 9780692544785

Library of Congress Control Number 2015954133

Vision Directives, Wilmington, DE

VISION|DIRECTIVES

# DEDICATION

*I want to dedicate this book to first of all my family. My lovely wife of 20 years and counting Roberta my best friend and partner.*

*To my children Vincent, Jeshale and Charity love you guys. To my father and my mother I love and appreciate you guys thanks for raising me and your abundant sacrifices.*

*To my spiritual parents Apostle Ivory Hopkins and his wife Minister Evelyn Hopkins and Apostle Levin Bailey and his wife Minister Rose Bailey thanks for raising me up in the teachings of Christ and giving me a strong foundation and seeing the potential in me to be great in God.*

*To Apostle Larry Morris and his wife Prophetess Beth Morris thank you for leading me to Christ so I could start this journey called salvation. Love you all and will always be forever grateful. I will never forget where I came from because it has shaped me into the man of God I'm today.*

*I am truly who I am because of the grace of God!*

# TABLE OF CONTENTS

# FOREWORDS

I have served with this Man of God and his Wife for many when he was at Pilgrims Ministry of Deliverance. I believe that God has called this Apostle/Prophet to impart, inspire and encourage the Body of Christ as well as those who are lost. This anointed book called. "From from Prison to the Pulpit" will remind that future Apostle, Prophet or Teacher that just because you been prison does mean you can't fulfill your purpose. Apostle Jermaine and Prophetess Roberta Johnson may God continue to bless you and your family.

Your Follow Laborer in the Gospel
Elder Therman Hopkins


*It is said that America is the land of opportunity. This is evident due to the countless number of people who forsake their place of origin. They throw caution into the wind and leave behind loved ones, friends, and a past. What is their motivation for this giant leap of faith? A shot at the American dream, or at best a fresh clean start. Unfortunately for some, like a bad odor their past follows them. We seem to live in a time where humanity, regardless of ethnicity or geographical location, is fascinated with airing out others dirty laundry. We have waged a war on one another using the past as ammunition. The reward you ask? The self-righteous satisfaction of saying that once a bad choice is made, that it defines who you are. Apostle Paul told the church in 2 Corinthians 5:17 that any man*

i

*that is in Christ is a new creature, and that the old is gone and all things are new. This does not mean that things never happened. It means that underneath the poor choices the image and likeness of God still exists and is waiting to be renewed. In this book you will go along on a journey with Prophet Jermaine Johnson, as he takes inside his life. The circumstances, the choices, and the deceitfulness of sin that led to incarceration. He will also share how the very place satan intended to destroy him, initiated his encounter with Jesus Christ. This merciful encounter leads us to present day, where Prophet Johnson is now Pastor, author, and spokesman for the kingdom of God. With Biblical revelation, and personal transparent truth, this book will encourage you and testify that with God all things are possible, and that even you can go from the prison to the pulpit.*

*Jason Hall*

*"He who the Son sets free is free indeed."*

# INTRODUCTION

I'm writing this book about my life because I'm not ashamed of the gospel of Jesus Christ because it is the power of God unto salvation. I was once a prisoner in prison who now stands in the pulpit preaching the Word of God. I'm now a willing prisoner of Christ. I'm sold out to do his will for my life which includes service towards other people. I'm allowing you all who read this book to go on the journey with me as I go through my whole life and show how far God has brought me and is bringing me as I honor his Son Jesus Christ. We all have a testimony. We overcome the enemy by the blood of Jesus Christ the Lamb of God and by the word of our testimony. My prayer is that my testimony will inspire others to overcome and reach their full potential in Christ. May all who read this book be truly blessed and encouraged to keep moving forward in God and know in him we can do anything because all things are possible to them that believe. There is an ex-convict out there and I want you to know you are not just an assigned SBI number given to you by your state prison system but you are somebody to Christ and you have the potential to walk in greatness. May God truly inspire and bring his best out of you. I truly know beyond a shadow of a doubt that God can change anybody and I do mean anybody. I know this because He truly changed me. I a living witness about the power of God that can turn you into another man. I have made many mistakes before Christ and I have made a few after Christ and I continue to fall short of His glory but because of God's love for me I refuse to give up or go back. God has put can't turn back in my heart and spirit and my future is looking better and better every day. As we go on this journey together about my life my pray is someone will find hope and know God has a great plan for your life but He needs your cooperation to get it done. He does it in us and with us not without us. I want to tell some young drug dealer out there that you don't have to do what you are doing because I know a God who can and will bless you if you just receive Him and believe Him then he will give you the power to change. You see I use to be a so called thug but now I engulfed in His love and now I'm a soldier in the army of the Lord and my head General Jesus Christ has given me orders to lead people to salvation and touch lives through my testimony. Be blessed as we explore my life and I take the covers off so you can truly see how far the Lord has brought me and I have come.

# IN THE BEGINNING

I was born on March 11, 1973 on a Sunday morning in Seaford, DE to my unwed parents. My father was in his early twenties and my mother a teenager. I don't remember a lot before the age of about five but we were a family of four. It was me my parents and my sister, who is two years younger than myself. I know my parents were not devout church people but more of the partying type. We did go to church occasionally, on some Easter Sunday's and at times when our mother would ship us off to go to Sunday school at the Church of God in Seaford. I was never really churched as a child but my mother did teach us to pray, "Now I lay me down to sleep" every night and she had a big white bible with pictures that she used to recite Psalms 23.

We did move from time to time because my parents

frequently separated. I do remember at about the age of five we lived in this big white two-story house that was down the end of a long dirt road. I had a huge box full of toys including drums and an organ. I remember one night the house caught fire. We had a wood stove at that time and somehow it exploded and the house caught on fire. We had to escape from the 2nd story because the fire started down stairs and was rising upstairs where all our bedrooms were. Thank God we all escaped unharmed.

There were also hard financial situations that caused us to have to move at various times. My parents did get married about two years after I was born and before my sister was born. Like I mentioned, there were many times of separation between my parents. My sister and I lived with each parent at different times during our adolescent years but mostly with our mother. During my childhood I was always into things like climbing trees, jumping off the roof, hiding under houses and in fields. I also ventured into trying to kill cats with bb guns. I was into all kinds of mischievous things. I even remember my sister and I setting fields on fire. Luckily we put them out before they got out of hand and of course I played doctor and house with the girls next door.

One summer vacation while visiting with cousins in Wilmington, DE we spotted some little kids coming from church with nice clothes on and we would hit them with water balloons. We were truly full of mischief back then. My parents were usually busy on the weekend playing cards, drinking alcohol and partying, like most people did after a full work week. On occasion they would go out and party but when they came home is when the fighting would begin. I don't just mean arguing but actual physical fighting. My sister and I lived in fear a lot because we didn't know whether someone, especially our mother, would be severely harmed or even killed. I want to say these types of situations are very damaging to children. Sometimes these mental pictures follow you throughout your whole life.

My father was my role model. He was also the one that gave me my first sip of beer and let me watch, on occasion, those late movies. You know the ones with the naked women on the screen. My mother would try to cover my eyes but my father would say, "aww let him see it. He has to see it sometime or another."

I remember crabbing at the crabbing pier called Strawberry Landing and I was looking for my dad and couldn't find him. When I did see him he was looking at something. I began to look in the direction he was looking and I saw what he saw - women in bathing suits in a boat. I was looking so hard and walking that I walked right off the pier into the water. Some older guy got me out and I ran to the car and locked all the doors. I didn't realize then but I know now that was one of my first encounters with lust. I'm being transparent because sometimes we create patterns in our lives that start in our childhood. Thank God, no matter where we come from or where we have been God has the power to set us free if we believe in and receive his Son Jesus Christ.

I remember our family settling down in a little green house with blue shutters in an area of Seaford called Concord. This is where I would spend the majority of my teenage years. This would also be the same house where I would end up being escorted out in handcuffs. Most people would think of good things when they think about where they grew up but for me, at times it was almost like a nightmare.

I want to take you back to those adolescent years so you can have a look through my eyes and see things the way I saw them. Other members of my family may have seen it differently but this is my testimony and how I viewed it.

I'm telling my testimony because someone out there needs to hear this. They believe due to growing up in a tough environment that they are a product of that environment. I'm here to encourage you and let you know that you don't have to be. Many of us have grown up in disorganized and dysfunctional families but there is hope and there is a future when you have a relationship with Christ. He can turn anyone around and make their life successful. So don't allow the devil to tell you that because you have been in bad situations in life that nothing can change. I'm here to tell you today that he is a liar and my savior Jesus Christ can take you from whatsoever prison of bondage you may be in and bring you into the freedom of being in His presence. In His presence is the fullness of joy and at His right hand pleasures forevermore.

Now let's explore when the Lord brought a miraculous healing in my life. I want all who read this to know that my God is a healing God and of that I'm a living witness to His glory and power!

*"But He was wounded for our
transgressions,
He was bruised for our iniquities;
The chastisement for our peace was upon
Him,
And by His stripes we are healed."*

# THE HEALING POWER OF JESUS AND MY ADOLESCENT YEARS

When I was 8 years old my first encounter that I can remember with the healing power of God took place. I don't know exactly the day it started but I remember being in my school classroom and while the teacher was teaching it felt like everyone around me was getting louder and the room started spinning. Suddenly I fell to the floor and started shaking violently. I could hear the teacher say, "Jermaine get up!" Then she went into panic mode when she realized I wasn't playing. I had the tendency to sometimes be a class clown. She ran over and asked me was I alright. I could hear some of the other students yelling in fear. When the shaking stopped I had a knot on my head where I had hit the floor and the teacher and the school nurse escorted me to the nurse's office. They called my parents from work and I was taken to the family doctor.

This happened on quite a few occasions at school.

My friends were afraid of me and some of the kids didn't want to be around me because they thought I was crazy. There was one friend we called Tator, he would try to console me and defend me when others teased me about my sickness. He stood by me and I will be forever grateful to him for his acts of kindness.

Some of us as kids have been cruel to our fellow classmates because we didn't understand what they were dealing with. However, thank God he always has someone with compassion towards others in their times of weakness. The doctor finally diagnosed me with epilepsy. I would, at times have these seizures at home. I remember hearing my mother cry in agony one day as I was having one, "What is wrong with my son?!" and my father responding that he didn't know. The doctor put me on a medicine called Dilantin to control the seizures. I had cat scans, EKG's and they found no brain disorder or tumors. Thank God everything was normal. I was sent to a specialist because they couldn't understand what was going on. Then for some unknown reason my father said we needed to go somewhere. He took us to my grandparent's house - his parents. We went there sometimes but not very much. I believe because they were God fearing people. They had their own farmland and also raised animals and crops. We did visit them in the past when they would kill hogs but this time was different. I got there and they took me into the living room. One of my grandparents came down the stairs with a bottle filled with an oily substance. Which I now know to be anointing oil; Christians put it on people when they are sick. They use it to pray over them.

I then remember them putting their hands on my forehead and saying, "In the name of Jesus, let him go!" They commanded that spirit of infirmity off of me. I didn't realize what had happened at that time but I'm currently 42 years old and I have never had another seizure sense. I did not give my life to the Lord at 8 years old that would happen some years later but it was an experience that I would never forget.

At an early age I had come in close contact with the healing power of God for which I will forever be thankful. As the bible says about Jesus he hath done all things well. I know without a doubt that my God is a healer because I'm a living witness. I felt normal again. But it didn't last for long. The cruelty of children kicked in again and I went from be teased for a sickness to being teased for having long arms and certain facial features. They said I resembled a monkey. I had to deal with a lot of rejection in my life and that rejection led to bad decision making to try to be accepted. I want to say this, as I was teased I also teased others never realizing the pain I felt I was causing others to feel. When we don't know who we are we try to become what other people want us to be and in the process we lose our identity and our unique personality that God himself gave to us. Never, ever let people define you because that will corrupt the real you.

I also felt rejected by my parents because I was born

out of wedlock. I was made aware of that on occasions by the statements of other people. I also began asking questions because up to about the age of 11 I had a different last name then everyone else in the household and I wanted to know why? I want to say that no matter how a child is conceived whether by sinful acts or not, that child still belongs to God and he gave that child life because in him we live move and have our being. The children are the heritage unto the Lord. I don't hold unforgiveness towards my parents or anyone from my childhood for what took place because I can't hold unforgiveness and be free. The bible says, if we don't forgive others Christ won't forgive us, it is just that simple. I may have expressed and currently express some feelings I had or still have about some things but God has been too good to me to harbor hatred. On top of that, I'm free because who Christ sets free is free indeed. Now I must confess there were times I needed prayer or just had to vent out my feelings to some godly friends for encouragement and also without a doubt took it to Jesus in prayer. I want to be clear, I love my parents whole heartedly and I don't blame them or anyone for the bad decisions I have made in life. I made them and I had the opportunities to make better ones. I make no excuses because I'm not a victim I'm victorious in Christ Jesus. This is just my story of where God has brought me from and He has inspired me to share.

One major shock in my adolescent years was when I found out that I had other brothers and sisters. For many years I thought it was just me and my little sister. I remember some young guys would come to the house and my dad would send me and my sister in the back bedroom. He told us the young boys were church kids asking for money and we believed him. Then one day I was outside playing I was 10 or 11yrs. old then and while I was playing one of those young boys came up to me on a bicycle and said, "Where is dad?" I responded, "Who is your dad?" He then called out my dad's name. I said, "He can't be your dad because he is mine and my sister's dad." He responded, "Ask dad when he gets home." I ran to ask my mother because she was home. She told me, "Ask your father when he gets here because I don't have anything to do with it." When my dad got home we were sitting at the dining room table and when he sat down I asked him about the young boy on the bike and was that his son. He paused for a minute then said yes. I burst into tears. I was crying because my father had hid that from me and had lied to me saying they were church kids asking for money. I was truly devastated that day because my father, my idol who I looked up to had lied to me. I saw my father do many bad things in life from drinking to smoking weed to running women to abusing my mother verbally and physically but I still looked up to him. I still wanted to be like him but now I was crushed. I couldn't understand how he could lie to me!

I would not reach out to have a relationship with my other siblings until my late teenage years. I found out that my dad had at least six other kids besides me and my sister. I also found out why he never named me after him, because everyone was already calling me little Johnnie. Even my other sibling's uncles, that would visit my dad at times, would call me Little Johnnie. I didn't even know who they were at that time but they knew me. The reason he never named me after him because he had a son already with his name.

The crazy thing about it all was that I always wanted an older brother. In our house I was the older brother protecting my sister and there was no one to take up for me. I eventually moved past the pain of it all however it did have a tremendous effect on my life. It always had me thinking in my mind that you can't trust anybody because you will only end up being disappointed. One thing that being saved has taught me is that people are not perfect. That has given me the ability to trust again especially when they change for the better.

The rest of my preteen years were pretty normal and as I got older my parents partied less and went out less at least with each other. My father would unbeknownst to us head deeper and deeper into his addiction. He was going from drinking and smoking weed to trying and becoming addicted to crack cocaine. He would be gone for days and wouldn't come home at times. Bills would go unpaid and it began putting pressure on our family.

This is a powerful drug that has wrecked and destroyed many lives and many families. It has no respect of persons. I say to anyone who is addicted to drugs don't be in denial. You need help and I suggest that you need a Savior. I know an awesome one and the only one, Jesus is his name and if you would accept him in your life you will never be the same again.

Now let me take you into my teenage years. This is where things are going to get a lot more interesting and I myself would begin developing more bad attitudes and habits that would eventually lead me to be placed behind bars. If I could see then what I see now I would have made better choices and decisions but without Christ and good mentors it is very easy to follow the voice of the enemy.

# MY TEENAGE YEARS

I remember turning thirteen and thinking I was on top of the world because I was getting closer to being grown and living by my own rules, so I thought. I tried out for the Seaford Middle School football team and made the team. I didn't play a lot because I never went to get my physical in order to be cleared to play so I missed a lot of practices. I'd also go with a friend of mine to hang out around town instead of practicing. I didn't go get the physical because it cost money to go to the doctor and our family wasn't always doing well financially. It didn't really bother me anyway because I didn't feel like practicing to be honest. I hated discipline and to me practice was full of discipline from the coach yelling, "Run the play like I told you! We are going to run it until you get it right!" Or the amount of sprinting we had to do when we made mistakes in practice.

My friend and I would get back to the school just about time for practice to be over and we'd get picked up as though we had been practicing all that time.

I was pretty intelligent in school and that was not always good being a black young man in those days. Kids would label you a nerd especially other black children that I grew up around. They weren't very good at the school work so you were not usually a part of the so called popular crowd if you were smart.

I really felt rejected sometimes from my own race of people because of the photographic memory I was blessed with. I did have a big problem like most kids I hated doing homework because it felt like a waste of time to me. I got a lot of zeros for not doing it but because my tests scores were so high I still got pretty decent grades. When I did force myself to do homework I would do it the morning before school or in school during study hall. I believe I aced my test because God blessed me with a photographic type memory. Once I saw something it stuck with me. I was able to retain what I had learned in class and I was a good listener.

When I turned 14 I got my first job working in a watermelon field during the summer. I was chopping weeds out of the watermelon vines for a local farmer named Mr. Givens who lived down the road from my house. He really liked me a lot because he saw I was a fast learner and a hard worker, so he put me in charge of the other three weed choppers who worked with me. One of those weed choppers was my cousin and the other two were his pastor's children.

Mr. Givens even taught me how to drive. He trusted me with his own personal vehicles as well as his farm equipment. I remember on one occasion I got his work truck stuck in the mud in the field and he came out there screaming and yelling. I said to him I quit and walked away because I had my mind made up that nobody was going to yell at me. I had enough of that at home. Mr. Givens responded, "If Jermaine quits, then everybody is going." Later on the week he came down to my house, talked to my mother and she told me that he was outside and wanted to talk to me. I went out reluctantly at first but I went. We talked things over and we both acknowledged our wrongs and then I accepted my job back. During the school year when watermelon season was over I would get my next job at Skate World in Laurel, DE. Every Friday I would take down the petitions they had up for their daycare center during the week. Then I would put the petitions back up every Sunday. The doctor also took me off the Dilantin. I was on that medication until I was 14years old, even though I hadn't had a seizure since the prayer I got when I was 8. I was truly happy to be off medication and to be able to feel like a normal kid. The doctors had decided to wean me off the medication slowly by lowering the doses even though the seizures had stopped six years earlier.

The jobs that I had at that time were of course minimum wage which was about three dollars an hour. At that time it seemed like a lot to me. Every summer from the age of 14 to 16 I continued to work for the farmer Mr.

Givens. I also began buying my own school clothes and lunch. I felt good because I was taking care of myself a little bit, without my parents help. My mother took me to open a savings account at First Savings and Loans in Seaford, DE. I got my driver's license at the age of 16 and then I started working at Hardees in Seaford, flipping burgers as a cook. During the summers I would work at Vlasic Foods a pickle plant in Millsboro, DE during the day and Hardees at night. I worked two jobs because I liked making money and that was something we didn't have a lot of when I was younger.

I also had my first sexually intercourse encounter at 16. It was basically because of being pressured by my peers. They would say things like, "Man you still a virgin or when are you going to get some or I believe you're scared of girls." The young ladies didn't help either, because they would get close up on me sometimes and make remarks to me saying I was scared of them. I was scared to be real because nobody had ever really talked to me about sex. What I knew about sex I heard in health class or what I heard some of my friends say. That first sexual encounter opened up the door for me having sex with multiple young ladies because now that I had experienced it I wanted more. And I wanted it from whichever female was willing to give it up. I didn't have a steady girlfriend until I was about 18 years old because I never really saw a steady committed relationship in my family. At this time, before I get ahead of myself, I'm 16 and my father and mother were separated on their way to divorce but they lived in the same house and were both dating other people. My father was now even deeper in his crack addiction to the point that he was not contributing to paying the bills. I remember my mother sitting on the couch crying saying she didn't know how she was going to pay the bills. I was working but not making enough to contribute a whole lot. I told her I would take care of it. Some of my friends at that time were drug dealers and I decided to become one too and make that fast money. I would sell fake crack for a while which we called "flam" that I brought for two dollars off a guy we all called Fat Albert. I did it so I could make a little extra money. For some reason some crack addicts would be so high they didn't know real crack from the fake. At that time I also had my first bout with the law enforcement. When a friend of mine was throwing bottles at people in the road and it shattered the glass hit a young lady in the face and even though I didn't throw any in her direction but the opposite way, the fact that we were playing and throwing bottles at each other I took part of the blame for it. I remember the day I got arrested for it. I was driving in Seaford and got pulled over for a traffic violation. I believe I was speeding and when they ran my license the policer officer said that there was a warrant for my arrest. I was shocked! I didn't do anything! What was this about? They told me an assault charge. I still didn't know why. Then they said that is all the information they could give until I got to the court house. I had to drive to the court house because the only one who had a license in the car was me. So the police officer called another officer they boxed my car in and followed me to the court house where I was officially handcuffed. I was arrested for third degree assault. My parents came to get me because they released me to my parents care until our court date. We also found out that I was arrested about that incident with the bottles. When we went before the judge at court the case was thrown out because the young lady didn't show up to court. My friend who threw the bottle gave her money not to show up or can I say he paid her off.

After that I continued my lust for the young ladies. I continued to go from one young lady to the next even a couple of different sets of sisters at different times. As I was getting deeper in the drug game, I was about 17 at that time, and I saw my father buy drugs with my own eyes. I was in a Mercedes with tinted windows with some drug dealers from Florida. My friend who sold drugs to my father had the car pull up to my father's car to make the exchange. My father never saw me but I saw him. This was far from the days when he would by a bushel of crabs on the weekend and we would spend time together as a family. Crack cocaine was tearing our family apart and I was being drawn into the game.

My mother in the meantime would become serious with a man who would eventually become my stepfather. Sometimes my mother and (step) father would stay gone all night leaving my sister with me. I loved it I had a chance to drink, smoke weed and sneak young ladies over to spend the night. However, now I realize that I was doing these things to mask my feelings about the tearing apart of our family. I was hiding behind getting drunk and high and even being sexually promiscuous but I was really angry and hurting on the inside. I didn't want to deal with those feelings. I continued to party and I got away with it for a while without being caught. Until one time I came home drunk and threw up and my mother made me clean it all up. It didn't stop me, I continued sneaking young ladies over. When I turned 18 I brought a young lady over and lost track of time my mother came home caught me and embarrassed me by telling me to get this whore out of my house. I felt real low because the young lady was shocked by what my mother said. I said, "Mom you didn't have to say that." She said, "Take her --- home, get her out of here!" That is not the first time I heard my mother talk like that. I remember when I was 16 and an 18 year old young lady really liked me. We would talk on the phone every day. When my mother found out about it she snapped. She knew people who knew the young lady and I guess she had a not so good reputation. I remember the young lady came over to the house to visit me and my mom came out the bedroom and called me back and said tell that whore to leave my house she is too old for you. I went to tell her and she left crying and I never called or talked to her again. Outwardly I played it off but inwardly I didn't understand why it had to be done that way because her feelings were truly hurt and I felt bad for her. My mother and I argued a lot because different young ladies would call the house. I remember her saying that I was just like my dad. I love my mother and I know she was speaking out of her pain but it was true. I was becoming like him in my behavior and it didn't help to hear her say those words because that was the very thing I was fighting against. I couldn't defeat my dad's demons they were coming for me and they were coming strong. I now know they were family line curses that needed to be broken but without God that is impossible.

The summer before I turned 18 I had my second bout with law enforcement. My cousins and I were on our way back from Ocean City, MD. We were pulled over in Millsboro for driving through a development at 12 am by the Millsboro police. He stopped us and asked for identification. One of my cousins had left his ID home and when the police asked him to get out of the car he dropped three dime bags or $30 worth of weed out of his pocket. The police officer called for backup, put us in handcuffs and searched the car. They didn't find any more weed but they accused us of being drug dealers. I was a drug dealer but I had stopped for a while after a friend of mine got busted and at that time I wasn't doing anything. I definitely didn't sell weed, I sold crack. The weed we had we smoked we didn't sell. Anyway I told the police officers that they violated our rights by putting us in handcuffs and not reading us our Miranda rights. The officers huddled up after much discussion and decided to let us off with a warning but they took the weed, I believe, for themselves or maybe that was just my thoughts.

I'm now 18 and I have finally graduated from high school in June of 1991 and by this time my parents were in the divorce process. I was planning on going to the coast guard. I had signed up in school and was accepted because of the high test scores that I received. The recruiter came down and took me to a base. I would have went but when it came time for my physical I disclosed to them that I had seizures as a child and they said I need a written release from the doctor before they could fully accept me. The truth is I really didn't want to go after they showed me the basic training film of their new recruits so I went back home. After graduation I quit all my jobs, moved out of my parent's house and went to live with one of my older sisters in Bridgeville, DE in her apartment.

I started back hustling drugs right before I graduated. I remember the day I moved out of my parent's house. I had waited until my sister went to school and my parents went to work, then I packed up and left. There was no note, no phone call, nothing. I wanted out and I wanted to be free to do my own thing and that is what I did.

I began building a relationship with my dad's other children when I was 16. I started with my brother who was a year older and my two older sisters. I moved with my second oldest sister first, and dedicated my life to being a full time drug dealer. I could only do it part time in school but now school was over and I put off going to college. I was determined I was going to be a millionaire and this was my way to the top. I had been gone from home about two weeks and had not contacted my family at all but my father found out where I was. One of my sisters snitched on me and told him where I was and he told my mother. I remember my mother calling asking why I left and didn't tell them where I was going. To be honest I just wanted to get away from everything and everybody and live my life on my terms and I didn't consider or care about their feelings at the time. She was crying asking why I wasn't coming back to see them anymore and I said I would be back to visit soon. It did bother me to hear her getting emotional because it wasn't about hurting anyone it was about doing my own thing without any restrictions or being hindered.

My sister that I was living with said, "you gonna go back home." I can see it in your eyes after the phone call from your mother. I replied I'm never going back and I never have. I couldn't live with my family like that again. I have always felt like the black sheep in my family and even though I was the oldest child of my mother, I never felt like it because the spirit of rejection over my life would constantly stir up the feelings of being unwanted. I don't know if it was because I was born out of wedlock or because my mother had me as a teenager and that emotional bond didn't feel like it was there. I felt like I was the mistake that happened. I know people may do sinful things to conceive a child but it is God who gives life. Children are truly the fruit of the womb and heritage unto the Lord. My family was never the type to say, "I love you", except for my father on occasions but the other things he did sometimes negated that message.

My sister and I had a disagreement about the times I was coming in the apartment because she had kids so I moved out and moved with my cousin who lived up town. Now remember I left home because I wanted to be my own man without being told what to do and I was going to make sure that didn't happen again. I stayed there for a while until she put me out when her step sister, who I was supposed to be dating, caught me in bed with another young lady who she was supposed to be friends with. Needless to say, I didn't care. I was drinking, partying, selling drugs and doing everything I felt I wanted to do and not even considering the feelings of others. When you hurt and you don't get healed you hurt others along the way. It is true, hurting people sometimes hurt other people. I know because I lived it.

I moved out of my cousin's house because once again I would not be controlled by anyone and I moved back to the apartment complex, this time living with my oldest sister who I had stayed with from time to time. My sister was a crack addict like our father was. It was there that I began having sex with women in exchange for drugs. We called this tricking. It opened up a whole new level of lust in me. I realized the power I had as a drug dealer. These women looked normal they had jobs looked good and had their own places to stay. They did not look like normal drug addicts. When they ran out of money they used their bodies for drugs and I was ready and willing. I also began, not too long from that time, to form a relationship with a young lady who was also 18. She also was drug dealer and my live in girlfriend at my sister's house. We lived together with my sister but I continued to see other young ladies and continued to trick women in exchange for drugs. She would become the third young lady I would physically put my hands on. The first was when I was 16 and working at Hardees with a young lady I would have sex with from time to time. When I caught her with a love letter from another guy, although it was hypocritical of me, I couldn't take being disrespected like that. I know I was messing around with other young ladies even having sex with her and another one in the same night. She knew about it but I didn't care. I learned from my father that I can do things to hurt you but you can't do it to me. We couldn't take what we were giving out.

The second time would be when I was 18 and caught a young lady I was with in the bedroom with her bra off with another guy. I snapped and had the guy begging me not to hit him. I was dragging her by her hair on the floor yelling, "I'll kill you!" Again, I was not innocent because I wasn't faithful myself. I learned that behavior from my father that I couldn't take what I was giving out. Today I'm not proud of any of it. No man should ever, ever put his hands on a woman. It is wrong! And to all the young women out there who have a man putting his hands on you, I want to tell you, that is not a sign he loves you. It is a sign that he has a problem and needs some deliverance. Boy it seemed more and more that my mother's words, "You are just like your father", was coming to pass.

The next young lady that I was with was different than the others because she liked to fight back and even at times initiated the fight. I always said I would never hit a woman because I saw my mother's abuse but the demons in my father were now manifesting in me and the alcohol and marijuana didn't help. I wanted to be like my father when I was younger but only the running women part because it seemed cool back then. I didn't want the physically abusing women part. What I said I wouldn't be, I became. I want to say family line curses and generational curses are real and powerful especially when you try to overcome these strongholds without a relationship with God. We would fight constantly and I mean almost every day especially with my lust and alcoholic addictions. She would scratch me, kick me, slap me, and then I would end up choking her or I would get angry and go on the attack by slapping her and probably would have killed her if not for the intervention of my sister. There were times I went into a rage. My mind sometimes would flash back to the things I witnessed as a child and it was like it was being reenacted. I also found myself picking up another charge at that time for criminal mischief for breaking into another drug dealer's apartment who owed me money. It was me and one of my partners. We would break in steal a safe and then break back in and put the safe back when we found out that it had no money or drugs in it. The police couldn't prove we broke into the apartment so they just charged us for kicking in the apartment door. We had to go to court for it and we decided since it was a possibility that we may get locked up, we went to court drunk. I remember drinking a half of pint of Seagram's Gin. When we got there to the court we were informed that the charges were dropped because the drug dealer had got busted. We ran out of the court house and went to celebrate. Then in December 1991 my sister's apartment and another apartment down the street were raided for drugs. I wasn't there at the time for some reason my girlfriend and I left that day and came back later that night. When I got back I saw this white van at my sister's apartment from the other side of the street. I saw men in trench coats walking around. For some reason when the police raided the apartments they only blocked

FROM PRISON TO THE PULPIT

off one entrance and not the other. When I saw the scene I drove to a nearby apartment that a person I sold drugs to was in and hid all my money in some washing powder. I left my girlfriend there too. I threw my drug bottle over a fence and walked over to my sister's apartment. I asked the men in trench coats who were the detectives looking for, were they looking for me? Their answer was yes after I gave them my name. They grabbed me, took me inside the apartment, searched me, found something in my pocket, I was holding my breath when they pulled it out - it was a penny. I had a sigh of relief because I thought it was a piece of crack that fell out of the bottle I threw out. I hollered out to the detectives now you have to let me go. They replied shut up and sit down; which I did. One of the police officers talked to his boss who asked, "Did you find anything?" and he said, "No." Then his boss said you have to let him go and he did. I ran out of the apartment and I believed I kissed the ground. I ran back to my girlfriend's house, called my mom and then moved back with my father who was still living in the house I grew up in over in Concord. Unfortunately my sister and her boyfriend were arrested for possession of an unregistered gun that I told her to put up for me. She was playing with when they raided her apartment. Then a drug dealer friend of mine and his girlfriend in the other apartment were raided and were arrested. Drugs were found in their apartment.

My mother and sister were living with my future stepfather in an in Bridgeville, DE but I decided to go live with my father and his crack addicted girlfriend so I could continue my drug dealing business. You would think with that close call I would stop but it made me more determined to sell drugs because I thought I was smarter than the police. I focused my mind on becoming a bigger drug dealer and started drinking more heavily and smoking more weed. I smoked blunts. I tried buying what we call weight which is a major amount of drugs from local drug dealers but it didn't work out well. I remember trying to buy drugs from a new group of dealers from Florida who set up shop in Delaware. I went to meet up with them using my father's girlfriend's car that unbeknownst to me, was not registered at the time. I was stopped by the state police just as I was about to meet up with the drug dealers and a friend of mine. The police officer informed me that the car was not tagged and when he ran my license there was a warrant for my arrest for a gun charge and it was for that gun my sister and her boyfriend were caught with. The drug dealers were riding by as I was arrested and my friend jumped out and ran into the woods. I was taken to the Bridgeville police station, charged, then taken to court. I was allowed to leave after signing myself out because the judge said the police evidence was not strong enough to put me in prison. I basically denied that the gun was mine. I decided when I left the court house to go back to meet up with the drug dealers. My father and his friends dropped me off to their trailer and then rode around the block. I knocked on the door, they came out and then some of them jumped me from behind saying I was a narc. A narc is someone who tells the police about criminal activity for which they have some involvement themselves. I got up, left and jumped in the car with my father and his friends. We went back home to get guns and came back to confront the men that jumped me. I would have shot through the trailer that they were in because they would not come outside but my father stopped me saying kids may be in there, so we left. Those drug dealers became my enemies. They even threatened to take my life and told other dealers that I was a narc. Now no one would sell weight to me out of fear that I was working for the police. I guess I couldn't blame them I kept getting arrested and kept getting away with it. However I was just being set up for a bigger fall. It was funny, the drug world that had embraced me was now rejecting me. My girlfriend and I had also contacted a STD and had to take medicine for it. I got it because I was sleeping around and gave it to her. We got through that somehow and stayed together. She also had some family members that had connections to drug dealers in North Philly. We started going getting powder cocaine from there and her aunt showed me how to take make crack cocaine. So not only was I selling drugs but I learned how to make crack myself. I was back on top again bigger than ever. The people who I used to buy weight from were now sending people to me to buy weight when they ran out. My ego was big and people were calling my name again. I was feeling accepted. That spirit of rejection over my life was setting me up for a big fall. My family was even asking for my help to pay their bills which I would hustle to do sometimes. I bought my first car a Chevy Citation and I was off to Philly every other week. The car dealer forgot to take the dealer's tag off the car so I would use those tags to run back and forth to Philly. I even started working at a chicken plant for a while to take suspicion off myself. After a while I stopped going to Philly because of the fear of

FROM PRISON TO THE PULPIT

being caught. Some of my connections had got busted by the feds and I was robbed at gunpoint one time for a few hundred dollars. So I decided then to find a local drug dealer with big connections that I could buy my weight from. He would deliver the drugs personally to my house because of the amount I was buying from him. We also had a house guest, my cousin who had turned 18. I was 19 at the time he moved in with us in the house that I was staying in and now buying to own with the money I made off selling drugs. I went from making $500 a week to $10,000 a week.

My cousin was having problems at home. He was also trying out the drug game so I brought him in and showed him the ropes. I eventually quit the job at the chicken plant because my girlfriend didn't trust me around other women and I couldn't say that I blamed her. The lust in me was supersized by this time in my life and I was spending my days gambling, drinking, smoking weed and selling drugs. My girlfriend and I were fighting more and more. So much so that on one occasion the police were called. He let us off with a warning because I went to school with his brother. He said if he had to come back somebody was getting arrested and I was very afraid because I had a house full of drugs. Our fights got so bad that I went into a rage one time and chocked her until her face turned blue but it wasn't until after she had busted my head open with a mirror. She accused me of liking her mother because she knew I used to date her sister before I dated her so she thought I wanted her whole family. My father and cousin pulled me off her in time before I could have found myself with a murder charge.

When I drank I just turned into another person. When I wasn't drinking I would laugh things off. But when I was drinking I would go into rages. I was hiding my anger behind my laughter sometimes. I just wasn't very good at dealing with my feelings. One day my cousin who was trying out the drug game was selling out of my house while I was gone. I told him it was alright along as he had his own customers that he trusted. When I came back home that day I saw a white guy leaving my house who I didn't recognize. When I confronted him he pulled off. I asked my cousin who was that he said it's the new boyfriend of a customer of mine. I knew her because her husband would buy drugs from me and sell me brand new stolen goods. He'd sell refrigerators, stoves, riding lawn mowers, etc. I told him that guy looks like a cop. Did you sell to him? His response was yes. I screamed at him and said, "Man we are all going to jail now!" I didn't know how prophetic I was back then. After I calmed down I called a meeting with everybody in the house and informed them we were being watched by the police and they were trying to bust us to take us to jail. I knew there was an unmarked car across the streets at times and they (cops) would follow me when I drove around. I even outran them one night when they were following me. Plus crack addicts said that some informants who worked for the police told them the police were watching me looking for probable cause to raid my house. I was warned several times that I was about to be busted and I even had a dream about it happening but I never took heed to any of it. Why? Because the pride in me made me think that I was smarter than everyone else. The man who I thought was a cop turned out to be one and in December 1992 the swat team raided my house. They had probable cause. My cousin sold to an undercover cop out of my house.

We had just been out Christmas shopping the day before - spending hundreds of dollars buying gifts for everyone we could think of. I was lying down in bed late that day after a long night of drinking and my girlfriend was beside me. My cousin went to visit his mom and my father was in the living room. Oprah was on at the time and then all of a sudden I heard a "BOOM" at the door. I heard men shout out to my father to get down and then they proceeded towards me in the bedroom. I was shocked and stunned and couldn't move. I couldn't believe this was happening it was like being in a movie. My friends would even call me little Nino Brown from the movie New Jack City but this was not a movie this was reality. When I looked up men dressed in black gear had machine guns pointed in mine and my girlfriend's face. They said, "Stay still we are the police!" and wrapped us up with some kind of plastic ties. They took me in the living room and talked to my girlfriend alone. I asked was she alright she hollered back, "No!" They told me to shut up and called me and my father, boys. I got smart with the detectives for what I perceived was disrespect for my father. I was told to shut up again. They continued to ask my girlfriend where the drugs were and she told them where some of them were. They found the rest hidden in some washing powder. They brought us out after we got dressed and hand cuffed us. The police found some money under my mattress and said,

"We're going to eat steak tonight on you. But since it is Christmas you can keep the gifts and tell your family to come pick them up." My cousin was arrested near his mother's house. They had a warrant for his arrest for a rule 9- selling to an undercover cop. The police officers took us before the judge to be arraigned. While we were waiting for the judge they asked me to be an informant. They even brought in an African American cop to try to persuade me to become an informant. I refused and then they let me talk to my girlfriend who told me she showed them where the drugs were and told them they belonged to me and her. I hugged her and said we will be okay it's our first offense. I thought I would be mad at her but I wasn't because I know she did it out of fear and I felt bad for her. They read off the 7 charges against us and I was told we were facing 10 years. The bail was set at $128,000 cash each person. We were all taken to prison. I was singing a rap song called money and power. I was singing because I was trying to hide the fact that I was really afraid. Our families were crying as they hugged us and I said to them we will be alright. Remember I was used to getting out of stuff that I got into so why would this situation be any different? There are only so many warnings before destruction comes and this time it would turn out differently.

Somebody right now reading this book may think they are untouchable or invincible but they are not. We must remember, we will reap what we sow and I had put a lot of bad seeds in the ground of my life as well as the lives of others. Now I was about to be somewhere I had never been that is locked up without my own key for quite a while.

*"When a man thinks he is something when*
*he is nothing*
*He deceives himself."*

# MY TIME IN PRISON

Now I'm where I told my cousin that day we would end up behind prison bars. We had to take a shower when we got there and exchange our street clothes for prison clothes. We were in a barred prison cell with other prison inmates in a part of the prison called pretrial holding. I knew some people who were there and when we got there WBOC News was airing the drug bust at my house saying, "A father and son were busted in Concord outside of Seaford and a large quantity of drugs and guns and money were confiscated." I remember some of the inmates said hey is that you guys on television. I looked up to hear them say that a father and son's drug business was shut down tonight and all I could do was shake my head in disbelief because I couldn't believe this was really happening. I had to adjust to the prison life because things are different there. There is no privacy, it's like animals locked up in a cage. If I could say something to every drug hustler or criminal it would be prison is not where you want to be. We have to eat, sleep, shower and use the restroom around total strangers. When we did eat they would call out chow time real loud. I would spend some days in the gym to get my surroundings off my mind. I'd go to the law library hoping to find a way out of there through some legal technicality. We would get about an hour a day outside to walk around, play basketball, baseball or exercise.

My family had retained me a lawyer and I was offered a plea bargain of 3 years mandatory but I was facing 10 years with all the charges that were against me. I rejected the plea bargain and said I wanted a speedy trial. The prosecutor wanted me to turn state's evidence on the drug dealers who supplied me with the drugs. I refused to cooperate. The dealers I dealt with in Philly were no toys they would kill you and your family if they found out that you were setting them up to be busted. I refused and would not take a risk like that. I couldn't put my family's lives in danger in any way. I brought drugs for myself and sold them for myself so I took the responsibility for my actions. The prosecutor also made it known to me that he didn't like me. He told me that he hates drug dealers and even refused to shake my hand when we greeted saying, "I'm not your friend." I just looked at him and frowned and for once kept my mouth shut which at that time in my life was not easy to do. My cousin on the other hand decided to turn state's evidence on me to get a plea deal for his rule 9 charge -

selling to an undercover cop. He informed the police that I had connections in Philly and Delaware and although he met them before he didn't know how to contact them and that's why they needed me to turn state's evidence. My lawyer told me my cousin had made a video tape confessing these things and also saying he was selling for me. He did get out after making some type of deal with the prosecutor to testify against me at trial saying that he was selling for me which wasn't true. I just let him sell out of my house. I told the prosecutor that my father was just a drug addict trying to get high. They released him based off my statement. I was then asked to turn state's evidence on my girlfriend which I refused to do. She did decide to take the 3 years mandatory plea deal. After about six months of being in prison I went to what they call a preliminary hearing. It's a court appearance before the trial to determine if the prosecutor has enough evidence to convict someone of a crime. My attorney said he may have found a technicality that would cause the case to be thrown out. The police in their report never said that they acknowledged themselves before entering my home which is against the law. I was awake at the time and I never heard an acknowledgement that they were the police before they entered. The undercover cop that my cousin sold drugs to was on the stand testifying and he said he didn't remember if they did call out that they were the police or not. I then took the stand and when I was asked how I knew that the police didn't acknowledge who they were. I told the judge because the bathroom which was directly across from my bedroom had a window that was cracked open because we used a kerosene heater. I could hear everything through that cracked window which was next to the door they came through. The judge said he didn't believe that people had windows cracked in the winter time so I must not be telling the truth and then he said if they didn't acknowledge who they were he was going to let it go this time. So the charges against me were allowed to stand. On my way being escorted back to the prison the two guards said to me, "If you didn't bring up that story about the cracked window you might have been a free man. We believe you would have gotten off." Then they laughed. However what I told the judge was true and when I told the guards that it was true they laughed again. They said, "Come on nobody cracks a window in the winter time it's just not believable." I went back to the pretrial holding cell discouraged and not knowing what to do. I was finally in something I couldn't get out of and nobody could help me this time. Two months would go by and my trial date had arrived. I had now been in prison for 8 months. When I went to trial they offered me the plea deal again. My attorney suggested that I take it and I did this time. I remember my cousin who turned state's evidence walking by while I was in the holding cell and I hollered out, "Get him out of here!" They took him out of my presence and I was escorted to a room to sign the plea deal and then to the court room before the judge. The judge asked me was I sure I didn't want a trial and I said yes. The judge then accepted the plea deal and sentenced me to 3 years mandatory and gave me a $16,000 fine. He took my license and right to vote away. He said these words to me in front of my family who were in the court room. My mother and younger sister were present and in tears. He said, "You had a nice business going there Mr.

Johnson but it is over now because I myself and my police force shut it down. You corrupted the community you were in. I gave you that size of fine to be my first example of what I won't tolerate and you will pay every dime. You may have to get your family to get a loan to pay it and if you try to sell drugs to pay it I will see you again and give you 10 years mandatory." I was taken from the court house and back to pretrial holding until I was placed in what they call medium security in a drug program called RESHAPE that I signed up for that was a part of the prison. I was separated from the rest of the prisoners except those in the program. This was considered a rehabilitation program. I also started going to church and reading the bible for the first time in my life. The things I read in the bible scared me but I started to understand why I was where I was. It was clearly because of the things I had done. They would bring in different preachers to preach to us at the prison chapel. I never had a relationship with God just what you call jail house religion. I knew I needed to be changed but I was more focused on getting out of the physical prison itself and not realizing that the imprisonment of my soul was more detrimental to me than any other type of imprisonment. I met some Muslim followers in the program I was in and even started attending some of their services which were also held in the prison chapel. I was however discouraged from following that religion, thank God, because they were real militant and according to them the white man was the devil and everything was his fault. They also preached that black people were gods. However something deep down inside of me could not agree with this for one, I had friends that were white and two, I didn't believe they were the devil and we were gods. Now I know it was because I was taught just enough about God when I was a kid to know what they were saying was not right at all! Racism is racism whether it comes from blacks, whites or any other ethnic group. I also was turned off by their blatant use of profanity right in the chapel and their strange chanting like we were in Africa practicing some kind of witchcraft. The blacks are "gods" thing really turned me off. I asked, "Why are we locked up and why can't we get out if we are gods? Because the God I heard about was powerful and couldn't be confined to a prison cell and also wouldn't commit crimes." Of course I never got a clear answer to my question. All they did say was that we were deceived by the white man who is the devil and we didn't know who we really were. That just didn't settle with me because it just sounded like they were making excuses for why they did what they did.

In the program I did excel and became a leader and a teacher. I was given a certain level of authority over the majority of people that were a part of the program. We taught on things like decision making, personal responsibility, dealing with anger and other life matters. While I was growing in the program I met a fellow program inmate who was educated in criminal law and he told me he would help me get out of prison. He was also the head leader of the program. He told me because I was a first time offender it was possible to get my mandatory sentence modified but I had to go before a parole board to get their permission to be released. I was in the program about six to eight months before I received my letter of recommendation to go to the parole board. Myself and another fellow program inmate, who was white, we both went up to get our cases heard. They told me before I went that they would send a letter to inform me if they accepted or denied my request but they told me right there that it was accepted. Later on I received the acceptance letter and my fellow programmer who went with me was denied. I would be released on one condition that I go to the work release center in Wilmington, DE and enter the Crest program which is a drug rehabilitation program. I accepted and was transported to the Crest program within a couple of weeks. As I did in RESHAPE I excelled in the Crest program. Not only did I become a leader and teacher, I also got a job working for an advertising company and then a storm window and door company. The best part was I was allowed, after I found a job, to start going home on the weekends. I was so glad to experience freedom again even if it was to a small degree. The hard thing was every Sunday I had to go back to the Crest program. One weekend I went home with a fellow programmer who was on his first home visit and had to be escorted by a senior programmer. This is how I first got introduced to the young woman who would become my future wife. The fellow programmer was talking to his fiancée on the phone she heard my voice in the back ground and for some reason decided to call her sister. Her sister called the house and asked to speak to me I got on the phone we engaged in a conversation, exchanged numbers and made plans to meet up. We meet up a few weeks later at my mother's house in Bridgeville, DE. Our first face to face meeting was in a park. We walked and talked. We began talking on the phone more and eventually started dating. Our phone calls would last for hours but it would only seem like minutes. I felt like I had finally found someone who to some degree, understood me. However I wasn't used to being in a monogamous relationship. But with her something was different. This woman wasn't like any woman I had known. She was self-confident and she had established a life for herself and her son. We communicated a lot over the phone and our relationship began to grow. I began to feel like maybe this could be someone I could build a future with…someday. She even ate and cooked Christmas dinner with me and my family.

As time went on I began to spend my weekends over her house more than I was at my mother's apartment. She became my girlfriend and would even take me back to the Crest program on Sundays.

The day finally came, after six months that I informed the program director that it was time for me to be released. They denied my request at first saying, I needed more time to make sure I could make it out in society. They contacted the parole board and the judge confirmed what I said about being released after six months of treatment. One day I was walking from my living quarters at the Crest and the program director who was walking with a new fellow female programmer stopped me and told me, "Jermaine get out of here you have been released." I was so excited I hugged him and the fellow programmer and ran to call my uncle who lived in Wilmington so he could come and pick me up. It took him a little time to get me which felt like an eternity; only because I was ready to get out of that place. I was finally on my way home. No more unnecessary rules as far as I was concerned. My uncle took me to my grandmother's house where my family was waiting to greet me. They asked me did I want to stay with them but I was a 21 year old man now and I had already made plans to go live with my girlfriend in Millsboro, DE. My family wasn't pleased but I didn't move out at 18 to move back in now at 21. I wanted to be my own man. I was free now, so I thought, and nobody was going to stop the plans I had for my life.

Now let's open the book on my life after prison. It was truly an adventure and one I didn't see coming not by a long shot. God would eventually get the glory out of my life and I'm thankful that he cared enough about me to deliver and save me. God has a way of reversing the course you are taking in life and changing your plans to His. I thought I had the book written on my life with all the chapters in place but I didn't realize then what I realize now that I'm not the author of the book of my life. He made me, I didn't make myself. The decisions I made along the way created some bad chapters but He is helping me make a better ending.

*"When I was a child, I spake as a child, I understood as a child, I thought as a child: but when I became a man, I put away childish things."*

# LIFE AFTER PRISON

I'm finally free! No more prison, no more bars, no more people constantly telling me what to do! I only had one problem - I may have been free physically but I was still imprisoned in my mind and life after prison wasn't as easy as I thought it would be. There was still something missing in my life. I still felt incomplete. I'm now staying with my girlfriend and her son. I did have it arranged to start a job through the help of my mother and her boyfriend. I started working at Allen's Food a chicken processing plant in Harbeson, DE. I trained on days and eventually was moved to night shift. But my mistakes were still having a lasting effect in my life. I had a couple of situations, one I had no license and I was told by DMV even if I paid the fee to reinstate my license that I still had a year left before I could get them back, so I might as well keep the money until then. The second situation I had was the fact I had to report to a probation officer weekly and also meet with a drug counselor. I was able to convince the drug counselor that having a job and paying on my $16,000 fine was more important than meeting with the group and she agreed. She released me from the post prison counseling which was a mistake now that I look back on it. I wasn't as strong as I thought I was and I was moving way to fast. So when I started my job's first training on deboning chicken breasts, I failed miserably. I was placed where I would stack boxes and tubs of chickens to be shipped out. My boss loved me and I didn't mind doing that job. I was pretty good at it but is was nothing I desired to do for the rest of my life. Eventually I had to quit that job because it was hard getting to work at nights without my own car. I would at times drive my girlfriend's car but she and I both were afraid that I would get caught driving without a license and she had to be to work early in the morning so it was hard for her to take me and then have to pick me up. I would catch rides when I could but it just was not working out for me. Now I was in a dilemma. I couldn't drive or vote until those three years mandatory had expired. It seemed to me all that rehabilitation was for nothing so I started drinking again. I was under a lot of pressure because I wanted to prove I could stay out of trouble but instead, because I lived about a minute walk from the liquor store, convenience became stronger than my desire to do right. That is usually what I did when I felt pressured and wanted to get things off my mind, I'd drink. However once I was sober I realized that the problems didn't go away. I would drink on the weekends and sometimes during the week and by Monday when my probation officer tested me there was no trace of alcohol in my system. So here I was jobless and drinking. I could afford to do this because I had a little money stashed in my savings account and my girlfriend's Section 8 rent was very low. She also sold a little weed on the side as well as smoked it. I stayed away from the marijuana because I knew it took a long time to get out of my system. After searching for a couple of weeks I did get another job at Mountaire Farms in Selbyville, DE at another chicken plant. I was running the ice machine. I didn't start until the Monday after my birthday and I wanted to celebrate but this would end up being a big mistake. We started drinking early. My girlfriend bought me two 22 ounce bottles of Old English 800 which I gulped down quickly. I was feeling good, too good, and this was the beginning of a bad night because when I drank my whole mindset and the way I talked would change. Before I knew it I was drunk and cussing my girlfriend out at a restaurant. She had gave me her money from income taxes to hold for her and it was quite a bit of money. I got so loud and crazy in the restaurant that I left everyone in there and went to the car to lay down my head was spinning. My girlfriend came out to get the money from me to pay the bill. I gave it to her reluctantly and when I got out the car she jumped in, took off and hit me with the car. I was so drunk I didn't feel it. The couple that came with us picked me up. We caught up with my girlfriend and the young lady that was in the car with us got out and got in the car with my girlfriend and we followed them back to where we lived in Millsboro. I still was drunk and spewing out verbal assaults toward my girlfriend who was trying to ignore me. I then took her car and started joy riding around Millsboro with no license, drunk, and on probation. When I got back to the house she was leaving with the other couple I followed them to see where they were going. I was so drunk I followed them right to the Millsboro Police Station and by the time I realized where I was it was too late. You talk about crazy now that was crazy. I have to admit that myself. She jumped out the car she was in and police officers were standing outside. She told them I was drinking and stole her car. I jumped out of her car and told the police that she had been smoking marijuana. He talked to both of us and asked our names. I gave him a name of one of my cousin's because I was on probation. He then told me I was under arrest for underage drinking because that person date of birth I gave him was only twenty. I gave him my real name he then arrested me for criminal impersonation and let my girlfriend leave. I was sitting in the police station saying to myself here I go again, on my way back to prison. The crazy thing about the entire situation was the same police officer that stopped me in Millsboro when my cousin had those bags of marijuana and let me go then, was the exact same police officer who arrested me this time. I explained to this police officer that I gave them a fake name because I had no license was drinking and was afraid my probation would be violated when I have to report to my probation officer and I would go back to jail because I wasn't supposed to be driving or drinking according to the terms of my probation. They began to question me about robberies in the area and if I knew anyone who were committing them I gave them some false information about a drug dealer I knew but they said they didn't need that information. I explained to them I was starting a job on Monday and now I messed up. The police officer had a change of heart and said he would tell my probation officer that I was not drinking and they would release me without having to post bail but I would have a court date to go before the city of Millsboro judge at the local court house. I immediately called my mother who lived in Millsboro and as I was calling her I realized I still had the keys to my girlfriend's residence. As soon as my mother and her boyfriend picked me up I convinced them to take me over my girlfriend's house. My mother refused but her boyfriend saw the serious look in my eyes and he knew I would walk there even if they didn't take me. When we got to the house my mother knocked on the door and rushed in and asked my girlfriend did she want me there she said, "No!" but I asked my mother to leave. She left but not before saying, "if you get in trouble you are on your own this time." She told my girlfriend she was sorry that they brought me over there. My mother left and I started slapping my girlfriend a few times out of anger and then I wanted her to have sexual intercourse with me. I had seen this same behavior in my father when I was a young boy and here I was walking in the same family curse. I don't know why but the next day my girlfriend decided to give me another chance. She said I had to cut back on the drinking because it brought the worst out of me. I started my job at Mountaire Farms and we also decided maybe we should give church a try. I went to court about the criminal impersonation and the judge said I could lock you up for a year but I'm going to give you a break and he gave me a $40 fine which my girlfriend gladly paid. My probation officer, though reluctant, decided not to violate my probation nor send me back to prison. My girlfriend starting going with a friend of hers to a church called Trinity Holiness in the woods of Frankford, DE. I didn't go with her right away but I promised her I would visit on Easter Sunday a tradition I learned from my family. We went and the preacher was preaching. I thought he was talking right to me. I was like, how did he know I was doing this, but now I know the Holy Spirit was using him to bring me to a place of conviction of my sin. I didn't go back the next Sunday because I was still into drinking and enjoying myself. I wasn't ready to commit to going to church consistently. My girlfriend kept going every week. I did promise the preacher I would be back that last Sunday of the month of April. I kept my word and went back. I just didn't want to lie to the preacher. I gave him my word and I respected people who were serious about God. I did have enough of a conscience not to do that. On that day, April 30, 1995 God performed two miracles. The preacher was preaching and once again I felt like he was talking right to me. I didn't know whether to get up and leave or stay. I thought service was over after the sermon but the preacher started to, what I know now as, to prophesy or saying what God was saying to my girlfriend about her waking out of her sleep busting out crying because she was concerned about her brother who was addicted to drugs. No one knew this had happened but me and her. The next thing I knew she was at the church house altar giving her heart to Christ and crying. I was happy for her but scared at the same time because I didn't know how this would affect our relationship. However remember I said that there were two miracles that day. The preacher began talking to me next and saying I know when a preacher is talking to you like this openly it makes you want to go right through the floor. He then began to prophesy to me telling me about a funeral and how that funeral changed my life and how I had a hard time dealing with my emotions after that day. The funeral was my great grandmother's and he was 100% correct. It bothered me because she was the glue that kept the family together. As the preacher was talking so was the devil. He was telling me, "You are not ready to be saved this week because you need a drink and there are more women out there. Let your girlfriend go." But the conviction of God and the voice of God through the preacher overrode the voice of the enemy. Before I could think another thought I was at the altar with my hands raised up crying out to God and repeating the prayer of repentance and I could hear the preacher say this is a warrior for Christ. That was April 30th 1995 and I have never been the same again. My life has been forever changed and I won't go back from where I came. I will never forget that day or the man that God used to bring me into the kingdom. I have now been blessed with salvation and what an awesome feeling it was. I felt like something awesome took place on the inside of me that I couldn't explain. I just felt like telling everyone about it and I did tell quite a bit of people. I could finally truly say that I was free something I could never truly say before. My salvation was now a journey into a new life and that is exactly what it would be. I just couldn't thank the Lord enough for what he had done for me and I was very excited about it because something changed on the inside of me and the missing piece in my life finally was in place. I felt complete for the first time. I still was not perfect but I was progressing toward a new life and a new way of living. I could feel God's inner working bringing change in my life as I began to submit to his will. Everything was not easy but I had a feeling that it was going to be alright and I was glad to be saved and set free by the power of God. God truly does quicken you or can I say make you alive at the initiation of the new birth which we call salvation or being born again according to the bible. We are about to travel on a new journey together as I become the new creature in Christ that He had always intended for me to be in Him before the foundation of the world. So I invite you to come along as we take a closer look at my walk of salvation.

# MY SALVATION

We are now in my girlfriend's car on our way back from church and I turned around and said to her, "we need to make a decision because we can't live in sin. Either we need to marry or separate, you decide." When God truly saves a person something truly will change. I knew this had to be God because I was 22 at the time and I hadn't envisioned myself being married until about 30 but His plan is not always the same as our plan. The next day my girlfriend went ring shopping and accepted my request of marriage. We first asked the pastor at the church where we got saved to marry us but he thought we may be moving too fast and suggested premarital counseling. This was a good idea even though we didn't think so at the time. I want to take the time to say that premarital counseling is needed before any wedding is performed because there is safety in the multitude of counseling.

We decided to leave that church after attending for two weeks for that reason and because we believed there were too many church rules at that time. So two weeks after being saved we began searching for another ministry. A friend of my wife suggested we try her uncle's church called Pilgrims Ministry of Deliverance. When we got there we enjoyed the message. It was different because the preacher was more of a teacher. After service we explained to him our living situation and asked if he would marry us. He agreed but would be out of town that week so one of his assistants performed the ceremony. We were married July 1, 1995 just a few months after giving our hearts to Christ and after receiving permission from my probation officer. Although I was now saved I still had to deal with issues from my past. Due to my bad decision making I had to get permission from a probation officer to get married. After getting married we decided to join Pilgrims Ministry of Deliverance and become members of that local ministry. This was our first membership in a church since we were saved. We became active in the church after the leaders approached me and told me God had something good in me that will bless the church and that they would help bring it out of me. I started out helping at the altar and my wife would eventually work in the book store not too long after that. I also became my apostle's armor bearer. I helped him with prayer lines and made sure he had what he needed before he preached.

I also got a new probation officer because they told me I didn't have to come every week but now once a month. My new probation officer even said that there was something different about me and I expressed to her that I now have a relationship with God and attend church. She expressed she use to not care too much for drug dealers because of how many people they hurt just to make money but she wished she had more people like me who were not caught up in a cycle of going back and forth to prison. I was put on unsupervised probation after a few months and then completely released. Thank you Jesus! No more probation! My wife and I would serve for 11 ½ years in Pilgrims Ministry of Deliverance and grow in the knowledge and grace of Jesus Christ. When I got saved I had a strong desire to read the Word of God which was funny because I hated reading in school. I got away with it then because of my photographic memory. I could look over something and just remember it with ease. When I had school assignments I would read the front middle and end of the book to find the answers I needed. But when I got saved I had a profound hunger and thirst to learn about God and the things of God.

I received the baptism of the Holy Ghost a year later with the evidence of speaking in tongues at the same church, Trinity Holiness, where I was first saved. They were having a revival and I went to visit and during testimony service they were talking about being filled with the Holy Ghost and I stood up and acknowledged that I needed to be filled. They encouraged me to stick around after the preaching so I could receive it. I still remember that sermon it was called, "Ready to Rumble". After the preaching of the word I went to the altar, the preacher laid hands on me to receive and told me to thank Jesus for it. As I was thanking Jesus a funny sounding language came out of my mouth and I have been speaking in tongues ever since. At that time many people still believed in tarrying services or calling on Jesus until you spoke in tongues but it's about believing and receiving. I continued to grow in my walk with God and so did my wife. She was filled with the Holy Ghost at our home church during a revival. In addition to my son, God blessed us with two more beautiful children. We had two girls born less than two years apart in the same month. Marriage is truly an honorable relationship and to have children is truly a blessing and now I had both. However even with honor and blessings also comes problems, but with God on our side we will come through victorious if we trust in Him and His word.

# MARRIED AND OUR CHILDREN

I remember when I was younger there was a show called Married with Children. It was a show about a dysfunctional family who criticized each other often but showed some love towards each other at certain times. My family life was nothing like this show and we did have some bumps in the road along the way but we kept Christ as our center even in hard and troubling times. When I met my wife she was a single mother of an eight year old boy. Then I came in the picture moving in fresh out of prison not knowing how to raise a healthy family. We got saved married and then our journey as a family began. I have to admit it was a little rocky at first. Remember I said in the previous chapter that my salvation started out strong with a strong desire to read the word of God. My wife was truly born again however she was not in the word to the degree I was and instead of letting her work out her own salvation I tried to make her be just like me. In a relationship we should not want a robot or someone just like ourselves but a whole person with their own dreams as well as yours. This caused more problems instead of a solution in my marriage and family because I wanted to create a carbon copy of myself. I was also never a father before and now I've become an instant one. The relationship between my son and I was difficult at first because I thought he didn't respect me as his step father when I brought discipline and correction concerning certain behaviors and I believe he thought I was coming in to take over. Before me, it was just him and his mother with no real involvement from his natural father. We should have taken the advice of the preacher who led us to Christ and should have had premarital counseling but like a lot of people we figured we didn't need it and we thought we knew everything we needed to know and that we had it all together. That surely was a mistake because I believe as I said before that everyone needs to be counseled before they say I do. My wife felt I was overbearing when disciplining our son because he had never had a man who was actively involved in his life or corrected him on a consistent basis. She decided that she would handle the correcting of our son as she always had before I came in the picture. I felt like an outsider who was not appreciated or wanted and I decided to pack my bags and go stay with my mother who had moved to a trailer she and her boyfriend had bought. My mother eventually would marry her boyfriend who became my stepfather not to long after they moved in the trailer. They had moved to Seaford which was my hometown. I didn't get a chance to sleep there overnight because I heard the Lord say that I was running away and I needed to break the curse of failed marriages that operated in my family line. I then prayed gathered my things together and moved back home with my wife and I had also made myself a promise that I wouldn't live with my family again being a grown man now so running away from my problems wasn't an option anymore. I learned when I moved back home after my brief stay of a few hours with my mother how to pray more and lecture less. My wife eventually saw where our son needed instruction that only a man could give him. Being a little boy he desperately needed it. Then when we got that settled the problem then arose from his biological father because he thought I was trying to take his place as our son's birth father. I wasn't I was just trying to grow in God with my family. We would have some bad arguments with even threats exchanged and I had to do a lot of repenting at that time. We eventually came to the conclusion that we had a shared responsibility to raise a son and we would even learn how to be sociable with each other. While I was working on my marriage and raising a son I was praying for my own biological children to be birthed forth. I have always wanted children even had a few scares as a teenager but they never came to anything and thank God because I would have been an irresponsible father at that time. My prayers were answered about two years later when my wife stopped taking birth control and we would have our oldest daughter. This was an exciting time for me even hearing people say that she looks like me.

Less than two years later our youngest daughter was born in the same month our oldest was born and I was excited once again. I was present at both of their births and it was awesome for me but not so much for my wife because she was in a lot of pain. But after the kids came forth she was very happy. We also had just moved in our brand new house in Bridgeville, DE when our youngest child was born. I started a new job that year working at a scrapple company making Scrapple. It's a breakfast food called RAPA where I'm currently employed today as an assistant supervisor. Things were beginning to look up for me and my family. We were faithful church members and had become ministers. The kids were growing but our finances were not always increasing. The bigger the family the more it costs to take care of them and now we were a family of five. We were doing pretty good at first because my wife had a home daycare business and I had a fulltime job with benefits. Then an accident happened in my wife's home daycare business causing her to lose her license and her business. They took the license not because she was found criminally negligent but because the house insurance said she was not covered to operate a home daycare and because of my past felony drug charge. We lost the business and we were sued by the parents of the child who was injured for a $266,000 judgement awarded against us after they promised they were not suing because they were believers as well. We struggled for a while because we had an adjustable mortgage that all of a sudden almost doubled in the monthly payment. I still had my job but my wife struggled for a few years to find a steady job. It looked like we were going to lose everything we had. Our car was repossessed and we ended up filing chapter 13 bankruptcy to keep our house. I remember standing in my living room one day saying, "God what is going on?!" and He said to me, "Son, your purpose is greater than your circumstance." Also around this time we got a new edition to our household because my wife's cousin was placed in our home through emergency action through the state removing her for a bad situation involving her stepfather. My son was also a teenager at this time and both teenagers felt like they were grown so we had a lot to deal with. Our son had also before my wife's young teenage female cousin moved in had went to school saying I abused him physically. They sent out a social worker to investigate us and never informed me or my wife. That is how the school system works, even without any evidence to the claims being made, they will show up on your doorstep. The social worker for the state made a surprise visit investigated the matter and found that our son was not telling the truth. Yes I did correct him and even physically corrected him but never abused him. We explained to the social worker that we do discipline but never abuse our children. She decided from her visit to close the case after finding no evidence of abuse during her investigation. I want to say again we have never physically harmed our children. Yes we have corrected them but never abused them because we love them all. Even though the case was closed by the social worker I was devastated I felt like I failed as a father because someone from the outside had to come and question the integrity of our family. I remember sitting on the edge of the bed crying and my wife consoling me letting me know I haven't failed my family and we would be alright. I gathered myself together and I continued to be that God fearing leader in my home. You see you can't stop being a leader because problems arise or when your leadership is attacked or challenged in any way. I learned that sometimes we may weep for a night but joy comes in the morning. We would go on to still have family prayer and family bible study on Tuesday nights. After my wife's family member was put in prison then my wife's cousin went back home to her mother. The state had asked us about adopting her but the decision was hers. She decided to be with her mother and other siblings, so we let her go. Our son decided at the age of 14 that he wanted to live with his biological father. We went to court the court let my son make his own decision. My wife was devastated by his decision. I encouraged her the best way I knew how and told her sometimes we have to let go of the people we love. Some things did begin to turn around. The $10,000 that I had left on my $16,000 fine was taken back after I wrote the judge a letter and asked him to reduce it. He took the rest of the fine back. God is good! The $266,000 lawsuit was rescinded. We also came out of chapter 13 bankruptcy a year earlier than planned. God gave us favor with a credit union to pay it off and refinance our mortgage to a 5% fixed rate. Things were starting to look up again. I did have a few tragic situations during that time, my grandfather and one of my brothers passed away. I got through those times with the comfort of God. My wife, after going through several temporary jobs, started working as a temp for the state of Delaware Social Services where she would eventually become a fulltime social worker and now currently a senior social worker. Our daughters continued to grow as we raised them up in the church and we became deeply rooted in Christ and his church. After two years of being with his father our son wanted to come back home. It was not what he thought it would be with his father and his father's wife and that went both ways for all of them. His father and his wife had a hard time dealing with a teenager and at times even reached out to me and my wife about the situation. Our son stayed with us until he turned 18 and decided he didn't like our rules anymore and move out. He became a father of two little girls. He is now married today and he and his wife have four children. My daughters are currently both teenagers at this time one graduates this year as I'm writing this book and one is about to get her driver's license. My oldest is more serious about her education as my sister was and the youngest is a little ornery as I was as a teenager. They are both pretty good normal teens whose parents love God and happen to be preachers of the gospel. I thank God for my children I love them all. We have standards as most parents do but we don't dwell on their mistakes or at least try not to. We encourage them to do better and a little discipline never hurts. We teach them the word of God and encourage them concerning their own salvation because both the girls have given their lives to Christ but they each have their own journey with God and we are praying for our son. For the most part thanks be to God they have never been in any major trouble of any kind. Just a few bumps in the road in school for the youngest daughter and sometimes being around the wrong crowd for my oldest but overall God has kept and protected them and I'm grateful for that because they are truly his heritage because they belong to him. This is our family we have had our share of problems but we are still a family and through the grace of God we won't let anyone or anything divide us. My wife and I have considered divorce a couple of times over the course of our marriage (to be real) but those days are behind us thanks to some godly counseling. This year we will be celebrating 20 years of marriage and we love each other today more than when we began our lives together. Thank God that we learned through counseling and the word of God to forgive one another and move on as heirs of the grace of life together. I have learned and I'm still learning that I'm to love my wife as Christ loved the church and gave himself for it. She is my spiritual partner, best friend, lover and helpmeet. I always say we are like the dynamic duo. I'm Batman and she is my Robin. I truly love her and our children. God has truly blessed me with a wonderful family and I'm so grateful! We are such an awesome team together and God gets all the glory for what he has done!

# THE CALL TO TEACH AND PREACH AND THE PROPHETIC GIFT

My wife and I joined Pilgrims Ministry of Deliverance about a couple of months after we were joined together in holy matrimony. The ministry was unlike anything I had ever experienced when it came to church. They believed in and exercised the ministry of casting out devils. I remember being in awe because we could hear demons screaming out and fighting as they were cast out of people. I must admit it was strange to me at first and I was a little fearful because I had never seen that before. I kept coming to church however because the preacher/teacher was on fire for God. I loved the way he taught the word with straight up truth. He also had an assistant pastor who was on fire for God. They had different styles but they were both effective. I would often say that our church had a double portion when it came to leadership. I would come and sit in the back of the church building and just look and listen. Then one day the two leaders met me in the back of the church before I had a chance to run out the door. I usually left quickly because I just wanted to be saved and go to heaven. They said to me, "We don't know you that well but God has something inside you that is going to bless this church one day and we are going to help draw it out of you." They then asked if I was scared and I replied no but deep in my mind I was thinking, "Why are these men bothering me? Don't they know I just got out of prison and I want to be left alone and just go to heaven?" I left that day a little fearful but I kept being drawn back to that church week after week. One day a couple of months later, I was asked to assist people in the prayer line. Sometimes when people were prayed over they would become overwhelmed by the Holy Spirit and fall out at the altar. I also was my apostle's personal armor bearer helping him out with carrying his preaching materials, getting him water after preaching and other duties. I was doing this for a year and a half when I was asked to be a Sunday school teacher. I know I had heard God say to me in prayer come up higher but I didn't know he was talking about preaching his word. My apostle asked me to meet him at his home so I could get the materials I needed to teach the lessons. I was a little afraid but I went anyway. As I was sitting at his home with my wife he brought out some books and said, "You will be teaching from these." I took them and said what age group will I be teaching, assuming that I would be teaching children. He looked me in the eyes and said the adults. Before I knew it I hollered out, "the adults!" and he said yes. At that time I was 23 years old and the adult Sunday school attendees were much older than me. He then said to me son you can do it and encouraged me and said, "I ask you just not to be boring". I laughed and said I will try not to. I took his encouragement and began my teaching journey. It was not easy I had some opposition because I was replacing some of the older teachers and they were not happy about it. They felt like a young man was coming to take over their territory. I remember one time I got rebuked by one of the elderly ladies in the church for teaching that people needed deliverance from cigarette addictions. I didn't say they weren't saved, I said they needed deliverance. I believe they felt like, who does this young kid think he is? This elderly mother told me, "You don't know what you are doing. You have no right to say that because there are people here with that problem and you are judging them." I explained to her I wasn't judging I was just saying that God can deliver. When I left the room with the mother I felt discouraged. I felt like, if this is what happens when you tell the truth I don't want to do it. My apostle was walking by as I was coming out of the room and he asked, "How is it going?" I said, "not good" and I told him what happened. He said, "Welcome to the club." This is ministry and not everyone is going to be for you. I was surprised at his response. I thought maybe he would tell me how sorry he was that I experienced that. In retrospect I'm glad he did it the way he did because it taught me to be strong in the Lord and not be a quitter.

I found out that the mother who rebuked me was unhappy because I was her husband's replacement in teaching the class. My apostle knew that I could handle it and told me to get ready to teach next week. I did just that taught the next week and the weeks after that. I learned from that situation never quit even when there is opposition coming against you. Just keep pushing towards your purpose. I also had to forgive the mother who rebuked me and as time went by she told me I was one of her favorite bible teachers. Man talk about a divine reversal. The bible does tell us, when a man's ways pleases the Lord He will cause his enemies to be at peace with him. I learned from that situation to be consistent no matter what comes your way or against you.

The first time I knew I was called to preach was when I was teaching Sunday school and something hit me like a bolt of lightning. I started preaching about "where art thou Adam", calling men to their rightful place in God. All of a sudden people were coming out of the other Sunday school classes to hear. My leaders were glad I discovered the gift in me but they had to teach me to temper the gift and know when to use it properly. We then started a rotation with Sunday school. At first I thought I was losing my position but little did I know that my pastor (who ran the church while apostle was out traveling preaching and teaching the gospel) wanted me to become the head of the adult Sunday school department. I was also still armor bearer of both of my spiritual leaders. I was starting to also preach more inside our church and at other ministries. The Lord began dealing with me concerning my prophetic gifting that He placed in me and the prophetic gift that was in my wife. The first time I prophesied I was at home praying in tongues and as I yielded to God those tongues changed to English words concerning my wife and my prophetic purpose, destiny and callings. My wife would also begin her ministry training and the developing of her prophetic gift and call to the prophetic office. I would soon go from prophesying at home to prophesying in front of the church with permission and at times to individuals. My apostle would speak over my life concerning the pastoral and apostolic call on my life that would come to pass years down the road. Like anyone else I had my troubles in ministry but in those trying times we need to learn to stand still and see the salvation of the Lord. I didn't always agree with leadership and I had a lot to learn about ministry but I respected them embraced the vision and stayed where God put me until it was my time to move on. We must be careful that we don't move from where God planted us before our time especially during seasons of frustration. Frustration if handled the right way can become motivation to change. We continued to grow in ministry. My girls joined the dance team which they enjoyed. Then I began to notice something, sometimes when apostle and the pastor couldn't keep certain preaching engagements for different reasons they would send me in their place. They even sent me to a community event that involved all pastors and my name and my daughter's name was put in a newspaper article after a journalist interviewed us. I didn't understand why they were doing it then but I do now. God was preparing me for the pastor's position or office, as we call it, before I would actually become one. Over the years of preparation many tried to get me to start a ministry before my time even saying they would go with me. Some would even try to entice me by calling me pastor and saying I don't see why the leaders can't see this in you but they were wrong they did see it. It was about the right timing. God's timing. I still have not seen these people today as becoming a part of the ministry God gave me. I would always say to them, "God will have me and my leaders on the same page he knows what he is doing." I want to say again none of those people ever came with me when I started ministry, neither have they ever been a part of the work I'm doing for the Lord. Thank God he knows the perfect timing because when I was being pushed by others to go I was financially strapped and not able to take care of my own house. I would have been a burden and hindrance to the body of Christ.

God eventually spoke to my apostle while he was on the road one day telling him it was time for me to start my ministry. We would all come to agreement my apostle along with the pastor and I would open an account for the ministry with my wife and our tithes from about March 2006 to about October of that year. We found our first building in Dover, DE and Prophetic Kingdom Ministries officially started the first Sunday in November of 2006. Were upstairs in a 600 square foot building. I would call it our upper room. I was ordained my final Sunday at Pilgrims Ministry of Deliverance a week before and sent out to start a work. November 5, 2006 was our first Sunday as a new church. We didn't know who would be there or what to expect but our new journey with God would begin. We had handed out flyers in the Dover area with the help of some of the saints from Pilgrims. We just believed God that the word would get out.

# PASTORING MY OWN CHURCH

It is November 5, 2006 and we are starting the first service for the first time at Prophetic Kingdom Ministries Inc. All I knew for sure of who would be in attendance was me, my wife and my children. I'm excited but also a little scared because this is a new phase for me and my family something we have never done before. I was use to going to someone else's ministry and helping them not running my own. I was going from being an ex-prisoner who had spent time in prison now to a preacher preaching in the pulpit; not just every so often but practically every Sunday. Now it was my name on the door making me the one fully responsible for the conduct of the church body and what would go on in that building. Not to mention my life would now be on a greater display for others to see and the lives of my family. When we got there to start service some of my family members were there to support our first service and some new faces of people from the neighborhood in

Dover. My wife, my children and I sang praise and worship along with CDs and I preached my first message in our new ministry. The message was titled, From a Mess to a Message. It was about how God turned my life around. How I would go from the prison to the pulpit. One of my aunts was there and rededicated her life to the Lord in that service and so the ministry began.

We would have many visitors come through the upper room some would stay, and some would not. Some would become dedicated members who are still with me today. Some others would transfer from our mother church to help with the vision. Like all ministries we have had and have our growing pains or shall I say ups and downs. I was, for the first 1-2 years, the only adult male member and the rest were females and children. I had problems with my neighbors about the noise level. The landlord was willing to let me out of my contract because he said I outgrew the building faster than he thought. He congratulated me for being successful but the complaining business owner next door decided to move. We stayed there in the upper room for about 2 and a half years always knowing we were going to eventually move to Milford, DE. The lord also took me to the word in Luke 8:2-3 about how the woman ministered to Jesus of their substance and assured me he would add men at the right time. The Lord truly blessed us tremendously while we were there and for the first five years of ministry I refused a salary which helped the ministry to store up finances. True ministry is about sacrifices it is not about fame and fortune. I also continued to work a job until the Lord saw fit to do otherwise with me. In my heart I felt the Lord correcting me about the lack of men in the church. So I began to thank the Lord for his subtle rebuke concerning the lack of men and thanked him for the financial abundance and overflow in the ministry. It was however in my heart to move to Milford and God confirmed it through his prophets. A friend of ours from the mother church was looking for a building for her daycare business. She said the Lord spoke and told her that building was for me. She called my wife who called me and we set up a meeting to meet the owners of the building. But there was still about a year left on the lease in the building we were currently occupying. The Lord worked that out when we found another pastor who would sublease and pay me the majority of the monthly lease and the rest we would sow into his ministry as a seed offering for the year that was left. The new building had to be inspected by the fire marshal to become a church. For some reason the fire marshal made an early visit and failed the code of the building for a church. In the mean time I had put a picture of the new building up to inspire our faith to believe God for the new place. It didn't seem to be working out but then the owners decided to upgrade some things in the building to bring it up to code for no charge. Then the fire marshal wanted an outlay plan of the building exit and where the fire extinguishers were going to be. Those plans, done professionally, were very expensive and we needed the money we had to move and do some remodeling in the building. I had to preach the day I found out about the outlay plan and I was preaching about our faith being challenged. I told the pastor of that church about the outlay drawing that was needed and to my surprise, he said you can do that yourself. Something on the inside of me jumped. I preached that night, sowed my love offering as a seed back to that ministry, and I went home encouraged. The next day I got up, took some drawing paper and a pencil and drew the outlay of the building. I want to say very clearly art is not my gift, however, I did it and the fire marshal approved it. To God be the glory for all he has done! We met with the owner of the building again whose father was the majority owner and was in a Milford nursing home. They needed his approval to allow a church there and he whole heartedly agreed. So on August 8, 2008, we signed the lease to the new building. This was truly our new beginning. Some of our members were unsure about our move but most are still with us today.

Sometimes as a visionary and a pioneer in the kingdom everyone is not going to see what God is showing you but you still must proceed with His plans. Men started not only coming but joining the church. Some members decided to leave because I left the Dover area and that was fine. I still had to keep moving forward. We must always remember that we are to continue to obey God even when it doesn't please everyone. God was still and is still good to us. He blessed us by taking us from a 600 square foot building to a 2500 square foot building with a sanctuary area, mini kitchen storage area, dining area, and office area with plenty of parking. We are currently still there today. We are believing God to build our own building soon completely debt free. Like all ministries problems arise but we keep moving forward by the leading of the Holy Spirit. I have had times like any preacher where I felt like quitting and giving up the ministry. But thank God he has given me the strength to endure and I plan on enduring to the end no matter what because I love Him.

Please pray for leaders because many do give up, and give in for various reasons. I'm in the process of fully embracing and walking in my calling to be an apostle and I will be ordained on November 8, 2015 for this office which just happens to also be my wife's birthday! We are not just an ordinary ministry but we are a sent ministry that sends others to do the work God has ordained them to do. We are a multicultural ministry, made up of members with different ethnicities and social statuses. I have written a prophetic training manual that is already out and doing well along with this book and also some other writing projects I'm in the process of completing. My overseer and other prophetic leaders have confirmed the books and teaching manuals in me. God has truly put his treasure in earthen vessels so He can get the glory out of their lives. I give it all to him, Jesus Christ, because without him I could do nothing. Today I'm a person who went from a prison cell to a pulpit. I'm a preacher, author, father, husband, assistant supervisor, shop steward, and a child of the Most High God. This journey has not been easy but I keep fighting the good fight of faith and it has been worth it to see people set free delivered and inspired to walk in purpose and fulfill their destiny. I refuse to quit no matter the obstacle or opposition because I know that He that has begun the good work in me is able to perform until the day of Jesus Christ's return.

I'm thankful that God is using me, an ex drug dealer, womanizer, thief, etc. Who is now a prophet, pastor, and soon to be an apostle. I'm also an assistant supervisor and soon to be self-employed business owner. I'm also the chief shop steward that helps negotiate our company and employee contracts. I'm about to start my own radio program on a local popular radio station in our area 90.3 FM WDIH. I also have done my first radio interview about the prophetic manual I wrote and my first television interview. This was awesome because the last time I was on TV I was going to prison for drug trafficking. Look what the Lord has done! Both of my parents and my sister are saved now. My step father also gave his life to the Lord. He passed away from prostate cancer before I could write this book which has been hard to deal with at times but I will see him again when we all get to glory. We don't all attend the same ministry but we serve the same God. What an awesome journey this has truly been and I'm looking forward to the next chapter unfolding in my life as God reveals it to me. I'm excited about my future and also I'm excited about helping others find their place in the body of Christ. I'm truly without a shadow of a doubt expecting a great move of God as he has already moved me from the prison to the pulpit to preach and teach his holy word.

This is my testimony. To God be the glory, and all the honor, forever and ever blessed be the Lamb of God who takes away the sin of the world. I will serve him all the days of my life because there is nobody greater than him. I know that there are tests and trials ahead but they are not worthy to be compared with the glory that shall be revealed to us when we see Jesus in the day! Glory to God in the highest!

*"Trust in the Lord with all your heart, lean not unto your own understanding and He will direct your path."*

# THE CONCLUSION

It has been a pleasure sharing my heart and life with all those who read this book of my testimony. My prayer is that someone will be blessed and know that they can be something great in Christ because when we have Christ greater is he that is within us then he that is within the world. Remember we make mistakes sometimes in life but we are not mistakes. If God can change me he can change anyone. Never give up on your purpose and destiny because he that begun the good work in you is able to perform it until the day of Jesus Christ and he said that he would never leave you or forsake you if you are in Christ. Once again be blessed and be encouraged. God took me from the prison to the pulpit and is making me into the vessel of honor he had always planned for me to be. He told us in his word that if any man be in Christ he is a new creature and old things have passed away and all things become new. Man this has been truly an awesome journey and when I look back where God brought me from all I can say is that the Lord God is truly awesome! I say to all reading keep the faith and allow the master to make and mold you and I pray God's peace over your life. God bless until we meet again in another book!

Love you all, a faithful servant in Christ,


~*Jermaine Johnson*

*And so it happened just as the Scriptures say:*

*"Abraham believed God, and God counted him as righteous because of his faith."*

*He was even called the friend of God.*

# ABOUT THE AUTHOR

April 30, 1995 is the day we gave our lives to the Lord Jesus at Trinity Holiness Church. As with any growth experience there is a thirst for knowledge, with that we visited other ministries. A friend recommended that we visit PMOD where Apostle Hopkins is founder and overseer.

July 1, 1995 Apostle Thomas Sturgis presided over my wife and I in the GOD ordained union called marriage. During that same time we began attending Pilgrim Ministry of Deliverance where we became members. Through our union we have three children and two grandchildren.

Through faithful service I was soon asked to be the armor bearer for Apostle Hopkins and Bishop Bailey. I humbly accepted, and this lead to more opportunities for GOD to use me. Soon I began to teaching the Adult Sunday School class. I taught Sunday school for nine years during this time I began my studies as a minister. A year later my beloved wife began her studies as a minister.

As I studied, taught and served faithfully the Lord began to deal with my heart about Prophetic calling and the duties of a Pastor. The Lord's word was confirmed through his servants and church leaders. In 2006 my spiritual fathers' Apostle Hopkins and Bishop Levin Bailey told me to start looking for a building. We found a building in September 2006 in Dover Delaware. On October 22, 2006, I was ordained at Pilgrim's Ministry of Deliverance as Pastor of Prophetic Kingdom Ministries. The Ministry officially started November 5, 2006.

On August 8,2008 through the leading of the Holy Spirit we moved to the Milford, DE area into a 2500 square foot building which we are now in this present day.

# ABOUT THE MINISTRY

Prophetic Kingdom Ministries is a ministry of Jesus Christ with the purpose of ministering GOD's Kingdom (rule, reign, and authority) on earth as it is in heaven.(Mt.6:10) This will be done by the preaching and teaching of the Gospel of Jesus Christ the Word of GOD. This is for the main purpose of giving those who don't know our Savior Jesus the opportunity to come into the knowledge of his saving grace and to escape the wrath to come.

www.PROPHETICKINGDOMMINISTRIES.com

BOOKS AVAILABLE
On Amazon.com / Barnesandnoble.com /
PropheticKingdomMinistries.com

Made in the USA
Middletown, DE
06 April 2016